MW00948054

1

Blues & Rhythm Changes in All Keys

by
Evan Tate

Blues & Rhythm Changes in All Keys

Copyright & Disclaimer

The contents of this book are merely suggestions for practice toward your road to saxophone mastery. The author makes absolutely no claims for guaranteed results and assumes no responsibilities thereof.

Copyright © 2006 Evan Tate All Rights Reserved.

Contents and/or cover may not be reproduced or distributed in whole or in part in any form without the express written consent of the Author/Publisher.

To contact the author:

Evan Tate

www.evantatemusic.com

Blues & Rhythm Changes in All Keys

Table of Contents

Blues & Rhythm Changes in All Keys

Introduction

Welcome to "Blues & Rhythm Changes in All Keys". This book is designed for intermediate and advanced jazz improvisers to improve their skills in playing chord progressions.

The chord progressions found in Blues and "Rhythm Changes" can be found in just about 90% of the standard jazz repertoire. Mastery in hearing and playing these chord progressions can bring a large step forward in your jazz improvisation abilities.

This book contains what I call "Practice Solos" or "Improv Etudes". This is a technique that I have learned from former Miles Davis and Elvin Jones saxophonist Steve Grossman. These are exercises that are played in all eighth-notes, without rests. The purpose is to build up your "linear" thinking, playing through the chord progressions in a more linear fashion. The use of all eighth-notes without rests is to hinder that the practitioner of these etudes would just memorize them and then just play them by rote on stage.

I have used a variety of alternate changes in the exercises along with standard chord progressions in order to aid the practitioner to develop skills in "inside/outside" playing. A extra one to two choruses are left blank in order to write your own lines.

Why do all this? Learning and working through chord progressions in this fashion not only aid you to learn the progressions but to learn them intimately and to work out eventual problems.

Also, one concentrates on learning to play exactly the way one wishes. For example, have you ever transcribed a solo, or just picked up a lick from a recording? Maybe you've practiced this lick or solo over and over but the lines haven't yet crossed-over into your "normal" playing. Through the practice of "Improv Etudes" you can take the lick and set it in a practical context and learn it faster.

One can take lines from transcribed solos and pattern books like my **"250 Jazz Patterns"** and write them into an "Improv Etude". One can write an Improv Etude over a tune in a comfortable key and then transpose it to a more difficult key for the technical advantage and for the aural advantage – learning to hear the new key better.

It is my hopes that you will learn a lot here and will continue to use this method in the advancement of your improvising.

Evan Tate

How To Use This Book

To use this book I advise you to start with the Blues and at any key that you feel comfortable with. Start slow and gradually increase the tempo. What is very important is that you keep the "timing". Since the exercises are written without pauses, and that you do have to breathe, you should breathe where it makes the most sense musically and move on at the right place in the bar.

Keeping the time is more important than playing all of the notes!

In a "live" situation, the rhythm section is not going to wait for you to take a breath before moving on, so don't wait here either. I suggest using Jamey Aebersold's "Blues in All Keys" and "Rhythm Changes in all keys" or any other play-alongs that you may have or can obtain.

After learning to play the etude and that you have it pretty well under your fingers and in your ears, attempt to write a continuation of the etude with your own ideas of licks you've found in a transcribed solo from your favorite artists. Then, practice that.

After that's all done, move on to any other key you wish.

Like any other classically oriented etude, work on problem areas for technique. If there are any lines that you don't like – by all means change them! It makes no sense to practice lines that you wouldn't want to play.

After you've gone through all the blues, move on to the "Rhythm Changes " section.

If you have any questions or comments, please contact me at evan@evantate.com.

Have fun!

Evan Tate

Blues & Rhythm Changes in All Keys

Notes on The Blues

The Blues originated evolved from African song traditions from the multiple tribes of slaves that were kidnapped and brought to the USA from the 1500's. The song traditions were eventually influenced from European harmony. Jazz, Rhythm & Blues, Rock'n'Roll evolved from the Blues, and it still remains a part of the jazz repertoire of every jazz musician.

The foundation however stays the 12 bar blues with a set of 3 chords.

Most blues chord progressions are 12 bars long, There are also versions of 14, 16, 24 or more bar blues changes. There are many different 12 bar blues forms though. For our purposes here we will concentrate solely on the 12-bar form.

The tonic chord of a blues is a dominant 7 chord, a fact that doesn't fit very well in traditional music theory. The blues is not only about chord changes and scales, but is also about a certain sound, a feeling. Responsible for that sound are the blue notes: a minor 3rd, minor 5th, and dominant 7th notes. In fact these notes appear as part of the natural overtone series above the 6th partial.

For more information on the Overtone Series, go to:http://en.wikipedia.org/wiki/Overtone_series.

The 3 basic chords of a blues are all dominant 7 chords.

Here's a list of possible variations of blues changes:

Old "Original" Blues:

|| C | | | C7 |F | |C | |G |F | C | | (G) ||

3-chord Blues a.k.a. "Rock'n'Roll" Blues:

|| C7 | | | |F7 | |C7 | | |G7 |F7 |C7 |(G7) ||

"Swing" Blues (1930's):

#1: || C7 | F7 | C7 | | F7 | | C7 | |Dm7 | G7 | C7 |(G7) ||

#2: || C7 | F7 F#dim7 | C7 | | F7 | F#dim7 | C7 |A7 | Dm7 | G7 | C7 |(G7) ||

"Bebop" and Modern variations:

#1: || C7 | F7 F#dim7 | C7 | C7b9 | F7 |Fm7 Bb7 | C7 | Em7b5 A7b9 | Dm7 |G7 |C7 | ||

#2: ||Cmaj7 | Bm7b5 E7b9| Am7 D7 | Gm7 C7 | F7 |Fm7 Bb7 |Cmaj7 Dm7 | Em7 Ebm7|

Blues & Rhythm Changes in All Keys

Dm7 | G7 | Cmaj7 A7b9 | Dm7 G7 ||

I encourage you to listen to various blues recordings, not only those of the jazz genre, but also Rock'n'Roll, R&B, Bluegrass, and traditional blues recordings.

When writing your own "Improv Etudes" learn to use as many different variations as you can understand and that make sense to you.

For more information on the Blues, go to: http://en.wikipedia.org/wiki/The_Blues

Have fun!

Evan Tate

Blues in C

Evan Tate

Blues in G

Evan Tate

Blues in D

Evan Tate

x

Blues in A

Evan Tate

Blues in E

Evan Tate

Blues in B

Evan Tate

Blues in F#

Evan Tate

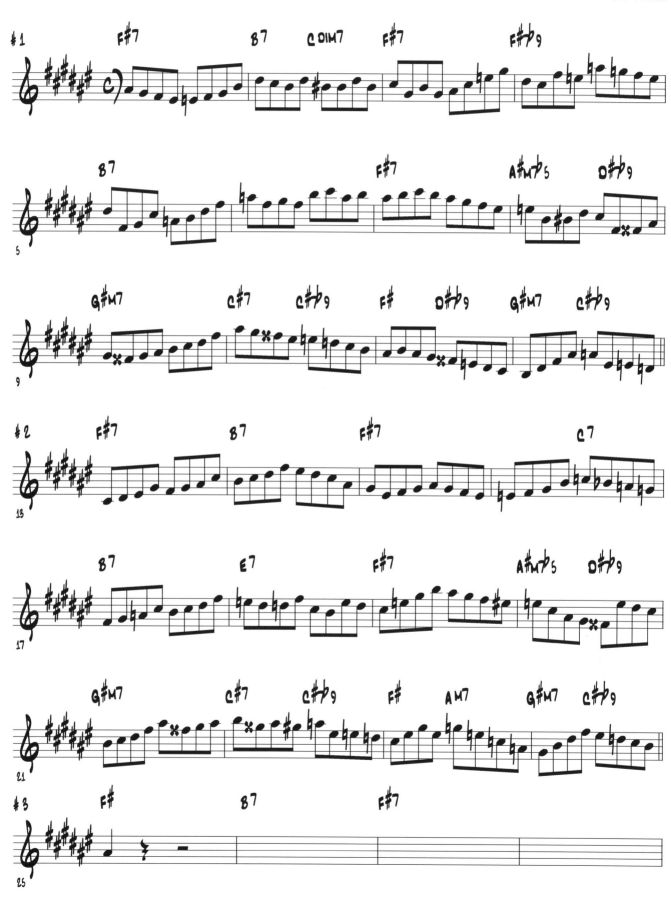

Blues in F

Evan Tate

Blues in B Flat

Evan Tate

Blues in E Flat

Evan Tate

Blues in A Flat

Evan Tate

Blues in D Flat

Evan Tate

Notes on Rhythm Changes

George Gershwin's "I Got Rhythm" is the source for one of the most popular chord progressions of the swing, bebop and hard bop era right after the blues progression. This form is often called simply "Rhythm Changes".

As with the blues progression, there are many possible variations on rhythm changes. Most tunes based on rhythm changes are played in the key of Bb, and are played at variety of tempos. These songs have a 32 bar AABA form based on the chord progression:

A: | Bbmaj7 G7 | Cm7   F7 | Dm7 G7 | Cm7   F7 | Fm7   Bb7 | Eb7 Edim7 | Dm7   G7 | Cm7   F7 ||

A: | Bbmaj7 G7 | Cm7   F7 | Dm7 G7 | Cm7   F7 | Fm7   Bb7 | Eb7 Edim7 | Cm7   F7 | Bbmaj7 ||

B: | Am7 | D7 | Dm7 | G7 | Gm7 | C7 | Cm7 | F7 ||

A: | Bbmaj7 G7 | Cm7   F7 | Dm7 G7 | Cm7   F7 | Fm7   Bb7 | Eb7 Edim7 | Cm7   F7 | Bbmaj7 ||

This progression contains many ii-V progressions. Any of the standard alterations described under ii-V progressions above can be used when playing rhythm changes.

Some common alterations on the "A section" are:

A: | Bbmaj7 Bdim7 | Cm7   C#dim7 | Dm7   G7 | Cm7   F7 | Fm7   Bb7 | Eb7 Edim7 | Dm7 G7 | Cm7 F7 ||

or

"C.T.A." changes:
A: | Bb7 Ab7 | Gb7   F7 | Bb7 Ab7 | Gb7   F7 | Fm7   Bb7 | Eb7 Ab7 | Dm7 G7 | Cm7 F7 ||

or

"Dominant Cycle changes":
A: | F#7 B7 | E7   A7 | D7   G7 | C7   F7 | Bb7 |Eb7 Edim7 | Dm7 G7 | Cm7 F7 ||

or

A: | F#7 B7 | Em7   A7 | Dm7 G7 | Cm7   F7 | Fm7   Bb7 | Eb7 Edim7 | Dm7 G7 | Cm7 F7 ||

or

"Coltrane changes":

A: | Bbmaj7 Db7 | F#maj7 A7 | Dmaj7 F7 |Fm7 Bb7 | Eb7 Edim7 | Dm7 G7 | Cm7 F7 ||

Blues & Rhythm Changes in All Keys

The „B" Section

The basic „B" section follows a dominant cycle pattern. Here are the basic changes and some alternate changes:

Basic:	||D7 | | G7 | |C7 | |F7 | ||
Bebop version:	||Am7 | D7 | Dm7 | G7 | Gm7 | C7 | Cm7 |F7 ||
Tritone substitution:	||D7 | | Db7 | | C7 | | B7 | ||
or like this:	||Am7 | D9 | Abm7 | Db9 | Gm7 | C9 | Gbm7 | B9 ||
or this:	|| Am7 | Ab7 | Dm7/G | G7 | Gm7 | Gb7 | Cm7/F | F7 \ B9 \ ||

Try your best to learn as many variations as you can understand and practice them in all keys.

Good luck,

Evan Tate

Rhythm Changes in C

Evan Tate

Blues & Rhythm Changes in All Keys

Rhythm Changes in G

Evan Tate

Blues & Rhythm Changes in All Keys

Rhythm Changes in D

Evan Tate

Blues & Rhythm Changes in All Keys

Rhythm Changes in A

Evan Tate

Blues & Rhythm Changes in All Keys

Rhythm Changes in E

Evan Tate

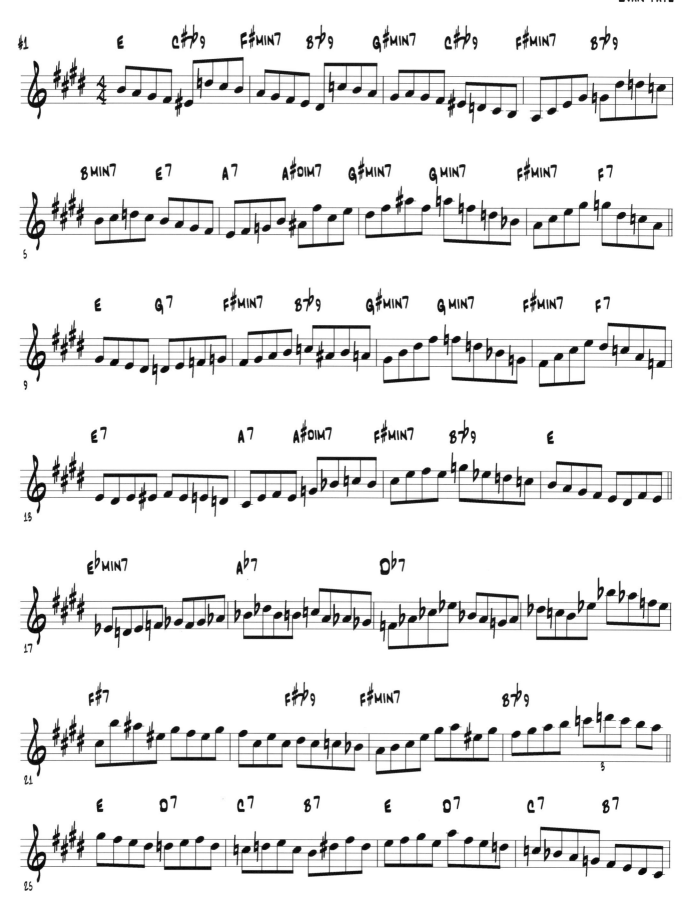

53

53

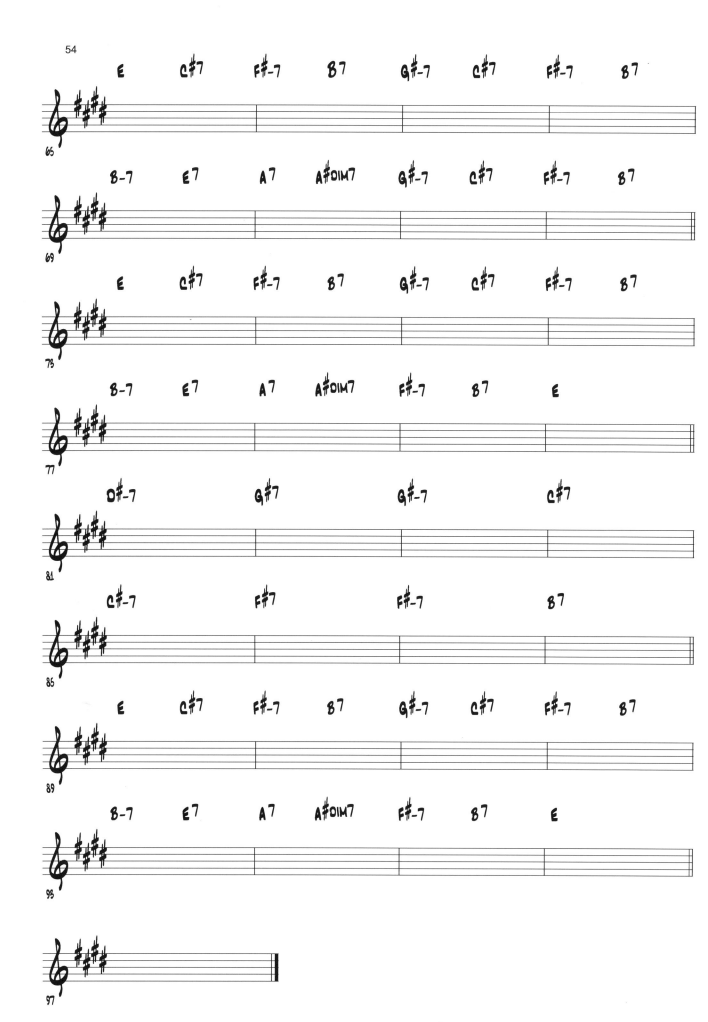

Blues & Rhythm Changes in All Keys

Rhythm Changes in B

Evan Tate

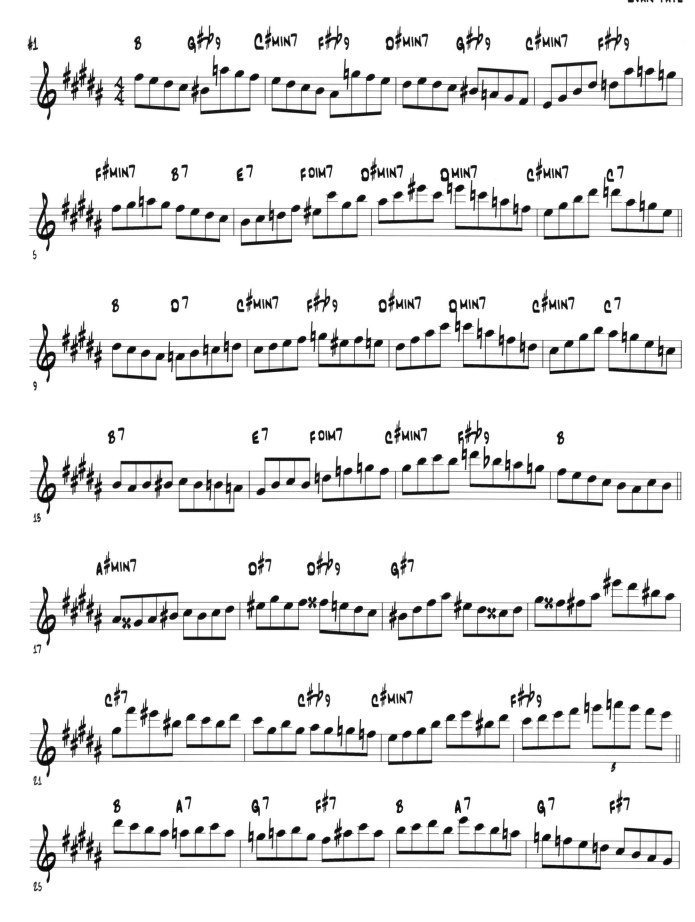

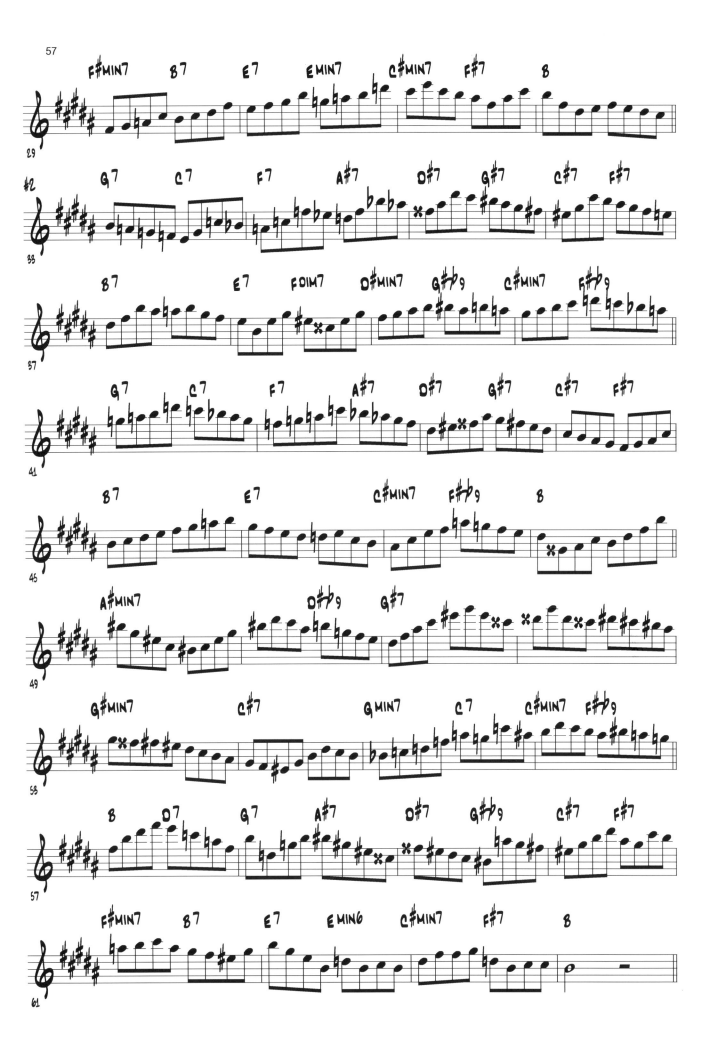

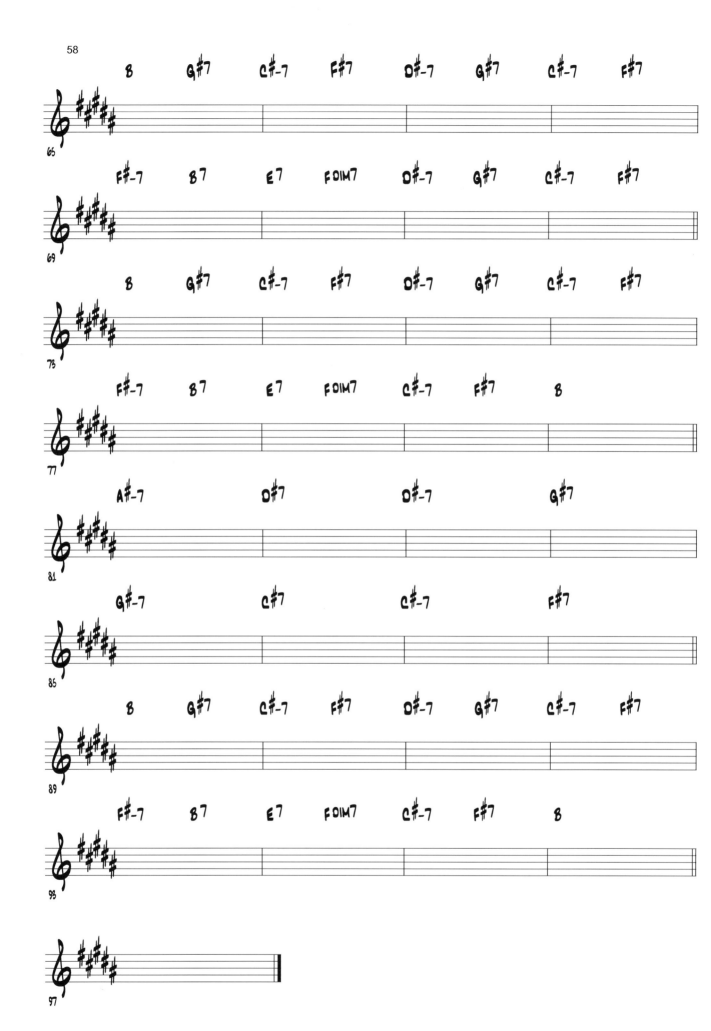

Blues & Rhythm Changes in All Keys

Rhythm Changes in F#

Evan Tate

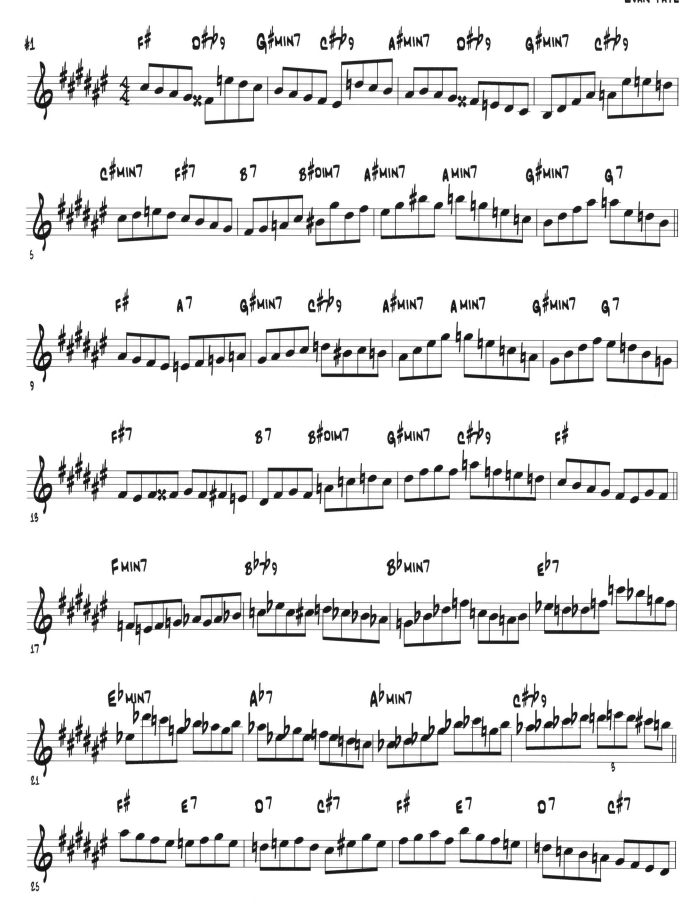

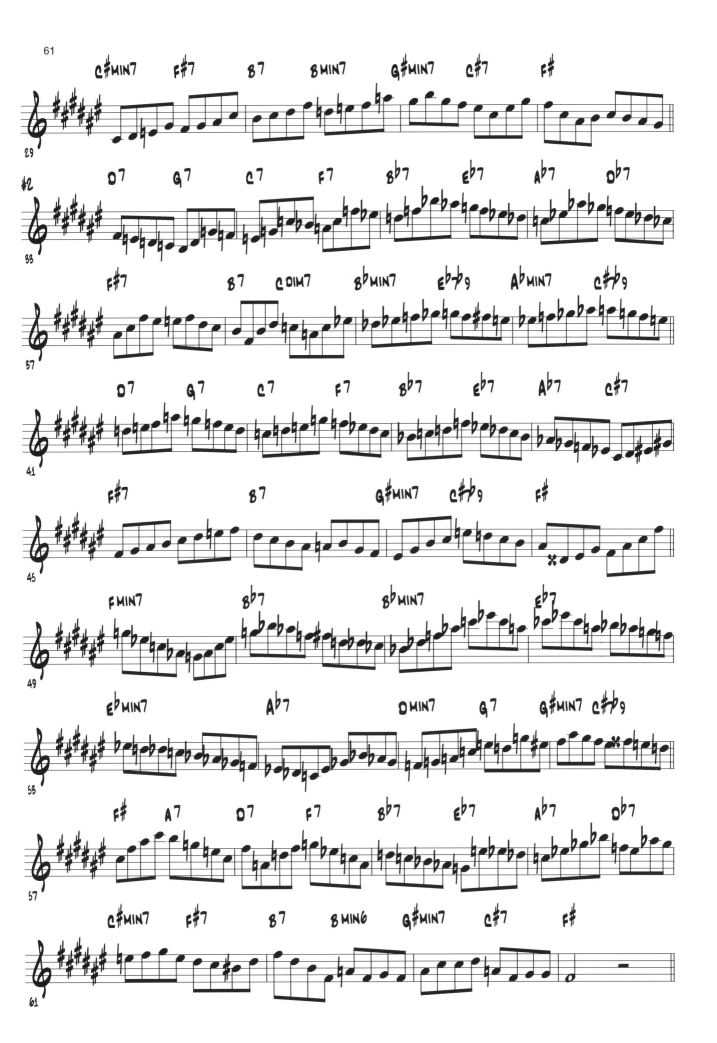

Blues & Rhythm Changes in All Keys

Rhythm Changes in D Flat

Evan Tate

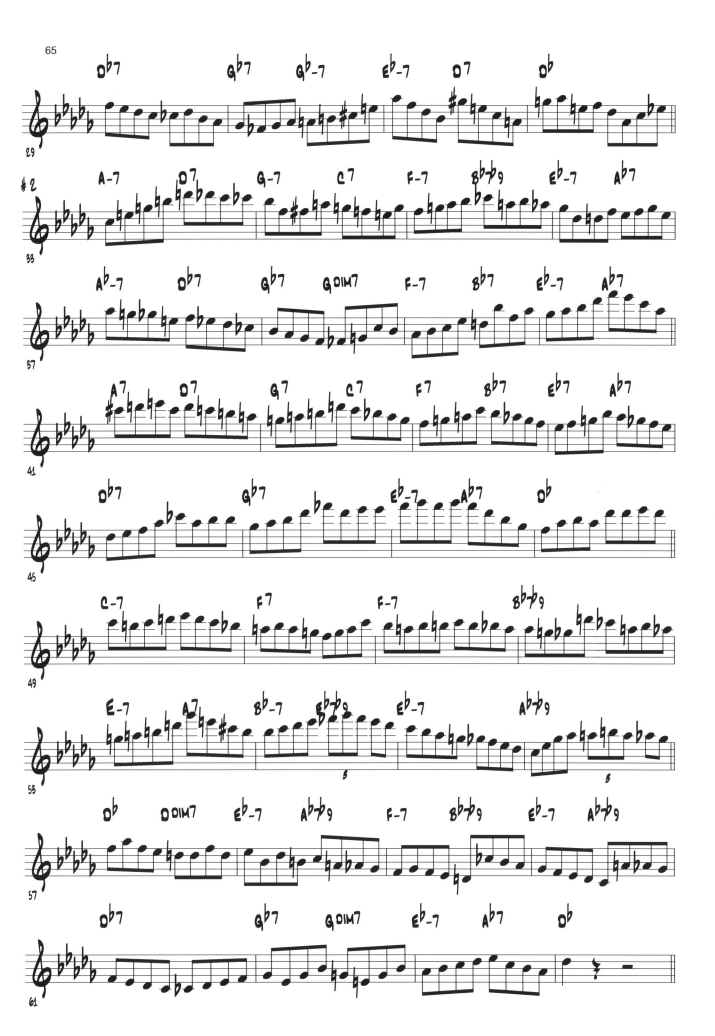

Blues & Rhythm Changes in All Keys

Rhythm Changes in F

Evan Tate

Blues & Rhythm Changes in All Keys

Rhythm Changes in B Flat

Evan Tate

Blues & Rhythm Changes in All Keys

Rhythm Changes in E Flat

Evan Tate

Blues & Rhythm Changes in All Keys

Rhythm Changes in A Flat

Evan Tate

Blues & Rhythm Changes in All Keys

Blues & Rhythm Changes in All Keys

Resources

The Blues:

http://en.wikipedia.org/wiki/The_Blues

http://www.pbs.org/theblues/

Jamey Aebersold's "Nothin' But Blues"

Jamey Aebersold's "Blues in All Keys"

Martin Scorsese Presents The Blues - A Musical Journey (2003) The History of the Blues: The Roots, the Music, the People

Rhythm Changes:

Jamey Aebersold (Vol. 47) I Got Rhythm (all keys)

http://people.uncw.edu/russellr/rhythm.html

Jazz Patterns:

"250 Jazz Patterns" - Evan Tate (www.evantate.com/shop.php) "Patterns for Jazz" by Jerry Coker

Jazz Saxophone Licks, Phrases and Patterns by Arnie Berle How to Create & Develop a Jazz Sax Solo by Arnie Berle

Way To Mastery: Saxophone Workout Book

About the Author

Evan Tate was born in the jazz captial of the world New York City in 1961. As a born and raised Manhattanite, he was exposed to music at an early age due to his parents, father Neal Tate and mother Marquita, both pianists and mother also a vocalist. Living on New York's Upper West Side he grew up hearing not only popular black music but also Salsa and Merengue. At the age of 12 he began studying guitar, alto saxophone and music theory. Shortly after he began to sing in the church choir and play in a rockband.

During his attendance at New York's famous La Guardia High School of the Arts, he began playing Big Band Jazz, composing and formed his first jazz quintet as well as playing guitar in a Top 40 band at age 15.

After a short stint as a jazz/composition major at the University of Bridgeport (Connecticut), he went on to attend the **Manhattan School of Music** (New York City) where he studied under the Master Teacher **Joe Allard**. During his attendance he also studied privately with former Miles Davis and Elvin Jones saxophonist Steve Grossman. Evan concentrated further on composition and formed the jazz-fusion band "REWIND" which he wrote and/or arranged all composiitons. By graduation he was a concert soloist with the Manhattan Symphony Orchestra.

Since 1979 he has freelanced with various pop, latin and jazz ensembles along many of New York's most in-demand session musicians playing in bands such as Jaki Byard's "Apollo Stompers", Roland Vasquez' "Urban Ensemble" and many more. Since 1984 he's been travelling throughout Europe with various Broadway musicals such as "Bubblin' Brown Sugar" and "A Chorus Line". He also freelanced on the music scenes in Munich and Vienna and tours throughout Europe with various bands including the "Munich Saxophone Family", Joe Malinga's "Southern Africa Force", Hermann Breuer's "Blue Bone", Joris Dudli's "New York Propjekt" and "Funktett", Wolfgang Schmid's "Manaus", "The New Doug Hammond Trio", his own projects 'Evan Tate Unit' and 'ET03', and has made appearnces in Austrian and German radio concerts.

Since 1993 Evan Tate is an Endorser for **Julius Keilwerth** saxophones.

Since 2006 Evan Tate is a member of the Jazz Saxophone Faculty at the **University of Music & Performing Arts**, Munich (Hochschule für Musik und Theater, München)

Blues & Rhythm Changes in All Keys

Other Products available at

EvanTateMusic.com

The "Way To Mastery: Saxophone" CD-ROM Products

Get a Private Lesson with me through my "Way To Mastery" CDs!
Each of these Lessons contains Audio Files (in the form of MP3-files, approx.60 minutes long) and
accompaning exercises to the lessons in Adobe Acrobat PDF Format.

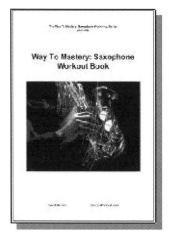

Way To Mastery "Workout Book" - This book is designed to give the intermediate to advanced saxophonist a powerful regimen to keep sharp on all necessary skills for today's saxophonist. Included in this book:

- Tone and Embouchure Exercises
- Scale and Interval Studies
- Ear-Training Exercises
- Exercises for the Extreme Ranges
- Altissimo Exercises

250 Jazz patterns - A valuable resource for students of jazz improvisation. Theses patterns start at the beginning level and move forward progressively to advanced and more complex patterns. PLUS: **"Practice Solos"** to help incorporate the patterns into your playing faster than imagined!
Available on CD-ROM or as a Digital Download!
Go to: www.evantate.com

Embouchure, Intonation & Tonal Development - This lesson will involve the theory and practice of an effective embouchure, a sure-fire method to improve your intonation, and the theory and development of good tonal quality. Many exercises are included and demonstrated.
Available on CD-ROM or as a Digital Download!
Go to: www.evantate.com

Altissimo Range: Preparation and Study - How to prepare and approach learning the range above high f#. Plenty of exercises are used to build consistency and great intonation.
Available on CD-ROM or as a Digital Download!
Go to: www.evantate.com

Made in the USA
Las Vegas, NV
14 October 2023

79113227R00048